GUNFIGHTERS

Osprey Colour Series

GUNFIGHTERS

Airworthy fighter airplanes of WW2 and Korea

Michael O'Leary

Published in 1986 by Osprey Publishing Limited
27A Floral Street, London WC2E 9DP
Member company of the George Philip Group

British Library Cataloguing in Publication Data

O'Leary, Michael
    Gunfighters; airworthy fighter airplanes of WW2 and
Korea.—(Osprey colour series) 1. Fighter planes.—History
2. World War, 1939–1945—Aerial operations
I. Title
623.74'64'0973 UG1242.F5

ISBN 0-85045-723-8

Editor Dennis Baldry
Designed by David Tarbutt
Printed in Hong Kong

**Dedicated to Brian Baird,
late of the Royal Canadian Air Force**

Front cover The spirit of the gunfighters. High
above California's huge central valley, an attractive
cloud formation provides a suitable backdrop for
history in motion. Ray Stutsman leads the pack in
his Curtiss-built P-47G Thunderbolt, followed by
Ellsworth Getchell in his RAN Hawker Sea Fury,
and Pete Regina in his North American P-51B
Mustang painted in the markings of 4th
Fighter Group ace Don Gentile

Back cover Heavy hitter: the squadron badge of
VMF-223, a US Marine Corps Corsair unit

Title pages Bill Greenwood's immaculate Spitfire
T Mk 9 two-seat fighter trainer is based at Aspen,
Colorado. N308WK is also pictured on pages
110–111

Michael O'Leary has been employed for a number of years as Editor and Associate Publisher for a large group of aviation-related magazines. Based in Los Angeles, O'Leary has had the opportunity to photograph many different types of aircraft—from the newest high-tech warplanes to primitive contraptions from the dawn of flight. However, his favourite aircraft remain those classic machines from WW2—the warbirds. Having photographed several hundred of these aircraft in flight, he is always attracted by the grace and symmetry of what were once deadly weapons of war.

Photographs for this volume were taken with a wide variety of 35 mm Nikon and Pentax cameras and lenses ranging from 18 mm to 300 mm. The photographs were all taken with Kodachrome 25.

During the late sixties, Los Angeles publisher and veteran pilot Edwin Schnepf became interested in a classic North American B-25 Mitchell bomber that had been a star in the movie *Catch-22*. Purchasing what had been the lead Mitchell for the movie, Schnepf set about to restore the bomber back to its original WW2 condition. Although the aircraft was flyable, its interior had been gutted of all military equipment and considerable repair and refurbishment was needed to make the airplane a reliable flyer. Several years of hard work went into the bomber and junkyards around the world were searched to find vital military bits and pieces.

The resulting restoration, named *Executive Sweet*, (right) became an immediate award winner and, in many ways, this single aircraft was responsible for beginning the trend of restoring warbirds as accurate representations of the way they flew in combat. Over the years, *Sweet* attended many airshows in North American and was always a hit with the crowds. During this period, *Sweet*—with its generous hatches and glazed areas—became a faithful mount for several aerial photographers who began, at first rather haphazardly, to develop the art of photographing veteran and vintage warbirds where they belong—in the air.

Some of the photographs in this volume were taken from the drafty, vibrating interior of the great old Mitchell, photographers slowly being deafened from the immense roar of the mighty Wright R-2600 radials. However, a number of other camera-ships were used to create this book: the Beechcraft F33A Bonanza, Beechcraft T-34 Mentor, Beechcraft C-45 Expeditor, North American P-51B and P-51D Mustang, Piper Lance and Piper Seneca. Lots of thanks is due for the skill of their pilots and especially to Bruce Guberman who flew the majority of photo-missions in this book.

Contents

Top gun

Left Phoenix from the ashes. Well, not quite ashes—North American P-51D-25-NA, United States Army Air Force (USAAF) serial number 44-73264, was nearly written off during September 1981 when it was caught by a gust of wind landing at Omaha, Nebraska. The airplane cartwheeled, resulting in extremely heavy damage. Utilizing many new and rebuilt parts (including a new fuselage), N5428V was eventually brought back to life over a period of several years

Above With the Rolls-Royce/Packard V-1650 Merlin just ticking over, the pilot advances the throttle just a hair to get the Mustang moving towards the taxiway. Bearing the famous insignia of the 4th Fighter Group, P-51D-25-NT N2869D, s/n 44-84390, survived a long and rigorous career as an unlimited air racer

One of the rarest of all Mustang variants is the A-36A dive bomber. Originally named Invader, the A-36A was derived from the early P-51A airframe and optimized for the dive bombing role (including the addition of dive brakes in the wing). The A-36A (which later reverted back to the Mustang name) was a spectacularly successful combat machine. Extremely fast down low (the A-36A was powered by the Allison engine which, due to a lack of efficient supercharging, lost out at high altitude), and more than capable of defending itself against enemy fighters, A-36As racked up many successes against the enemy and remained active until the end of the war. Only 500 were built and most of these were expended in combat. Fortunately, A-36A-I-NA, s/n 42-83731, survived to be restored in the early 1980s by Dick Martin for owner Tom Friedkin. The airplane is seen nearing the end of its restoration phase at Palomar, California. **Left** Pete Regina's P-51B poses in the background. Many parts for this restoration had to be manufactured from scratch—giving some idea of the amount of money and dedication expended by the owners of these classic machines. Now registered N251A, the A-36A can be seen at West Coast airshows

Few families can boast two brothers who are both Mustang rebuilders and owners. Pete and Angelo Regina both desired Mustangs but set out in different ways to obtain their own fighter. Pete discovered a rare P-51B wing, obtained a fuselage from an Israeli Air Force P-51D, and built all the missing parts. Brother Angelo, a Flying Tiger Airlines pilot, discovered a P-51D being used as a playground toy in an Israeli kibbutz. Both restorations have now been purchased by Joe Kasperoff

Preceding pages Beauty and the beast. Pete Regina's authentically restored combat P-51B N51PR in formation during the August 1985 Gathering of Warbirds airshow in Madera, California. This central California event draws some of the finest warbirds on the West Coast. Pete's wingman is Commonwealth Aircraft Corporation CA-18 Mustang Mk 23 A68-198. Now registered N286JB, the Australian built Mustang has had its aluminium skin highly polished and is painted in post-WW2 markings. N286JB last saw active service with the Royal Australian Air Force and then served a long period of flogging around the pylons at Reno as an unlimited air racer. The Mustang then went on to become a trainer for Piper's ill-fated Enforcer programme before being brought back into basically stock condition

Painted by a setting Florida sun, Bob Pond flies his P-51D N151BP. It is finished in 361st Fighter Group colours, and accompanied by his Grumman/Eastern TBM-3E Avenger in WW2 Fleet Air Arm markings. Looking at first like a Cavalier conversion (note the 12-inch fin cap atop the vertical tail) this aircraft was actually a 'homebuilt' Cavalier—being so modified by a private owner during the 1960s and even incorporating such 'updates' as air conditioning! Pond has recently built up one of the most impressive private warbird collections in the United States and has also started an aviation museum in Minnesota

Canadian duo. Surplus Mustangs from the Royal Canadian Air Force bolstered the American supply of P-51Ds during the late 1950s and early 1960s. Canada was soon stripped of the fighters, but recently more civil Mustangs have been brought back into Canada to feed the growing collector's appetite for the machine. Ross Grady is lead with his Cavalier-modified Mustang C-GMUS. This aircraft was obtained surplus from the air force of Bolivia where it had operated as FAB-523. Bolivia was supplied with a small number of Cavalier F-51D Mk 2 Mustangs during the late 1960s as part of the US Government's Project Peace Eagle (an incongruous name, considering the mission). C-GMUS was even assigned a new USAF serial, 67-22581, thus losing its original wartime identity. Ross's wingman, Richie Rasmussen's C-GRLR (rebuilt from the

badly damaged N5471V), was recently imported back into the United States for a new owner

Overleaf High over a wind-tossed sea, Hess Bomberger formates N6320T, P-51D-30-NA USAAF s/n 44-74497, with the camera ship. Hess, a WW2 Mustang combat pilot, has painted N6320T in the markings of one of the aircraft which he flew in combat. N6320T last saw active service with the Royal Canadian Air Force as RCAF 9230. Mustangs became the last operational propeller-driven fighters from WW2 for three basic reasons: 1) availability of airframes (many Mustangs had been stored); 2) high performance; and 3) ease of maintenance in the field compared to other American fighters like the Thunderbolt and Lightning

Bob Byrne and his gaily-painted *Rascal* are regular visitors to many American airshows. *Rascal* is another ex-Royal Canadian Air Force Mustang (RCAF 9270) and saw service with the USAAF as s/n 44-74774. *Rascal* was Byrne's first Mustang, but the '51 bug has bit hard and he has purchased several other Mustangs—including a very rare dual control TF-51D

Classics in formation. North American produced
the classic military trainer, the Texan; the classic
medium bomber, the Mitchell; and the classic
fighter, the Mustang. Fortunately, around two
dozen B-25 Mitchells are still flying and they
prove to be quite popular at airshows when flown
in combination with Mustangs. Bob Byrne flies
Rascal with Wiley Sanders' Mitchell at the annual
Breckenridge, Texas, warbird airshow

Top left Mustang C-FBAU, USAAF s/n 44-73140, was destroyed after a deadstick landing in 1984

Bottom left Brightly painted *Stump Jumper* seen low over the Texas countryside during June 1983 while being piloted by owner Jerry Hayes. S/n 45-11367 has a rather interesting history. Last serving in the West Virginia Air National Guard (the last ANG unit to operate the Mustang), the fighter was pensioned off at Norton AFB in Southern California where it became part of a small museum. A new base commander, having little use for 'old' aircraft, ordered the museum machines scrapped. Fortunately, Ed Maloney, owner and operator of The Planes of Fame Air Museum, rescued it. Years later, after another Mustang became fully operational, 11367 was sold to raise money for other projects. After stripping off layers of old paint, B-52 pilot Robin Collard uncovered the name *Stump Jumper*—apparently relating to a forced landing while serving with the West Virginia ANG

Above The powerful lines of the Mustang are well portrayed in this taxi shot of Don Davidson's beautiful *Double Trouble Two*. Davidson equipped N51EA (s/n 44-63507) with a modern IFR panel, including autopilot and LORAN-C for pin-point navigation. His 100 hours of solid instrument time in the P-51 is probably something of a record!

Overleaf Lockheed test pilot Skip Holm demonstrates the Mustang's gear sequencing on Jim Beasley's NL51JB. Note how the clam shell doors open to allow the gear to drop, the doors then closing to allow minimum interference of cooling air to the radiator

Above Against a troubled sea, Skip Holm makes a high-speed pass in NL51JB. A pilot's Mustang formation skills really show when flying with a much slower camera ship (in this instance, a Beechcraft Bonanza)

Left, right, and overleaf Canadian Warbird personality Jerry Janes has long been interested in high performance aircraft. Accordingly, during the 1970s, he had a P-51D restored from the ground up; the result is not only well-suited for airshows but also as a fairly practical cross-country machine. Painted in desert camouflage, C-GJCJ is being flown by Merlin engine rebuilder Dave Zeuschel over Southern California. C-GJCJ is now owned by David Price and registered N51DP

Following pages Mustang airpower at its best: Jeff Ethell flies Mike Clark's P-51D N1451D while Robb Satterfield formates in his N7722C (s/n 44-73420)

Big beautiful Jugs

Left Few shots could be more expressive of the size and fury of the Republic Thunderbolt than this tight formation being flown by John Maloney in the Curtiss-built P-47G and Steve Hinton in the bubble-top P-47M. During the 1960s, the Thunderbolt was virtually extinct from American skies but an infusion of six Thunderbolts from Peru along with several other complete restorations has brightened the situation.

Obtained in the early 1950s from a trade school, Ed Maloney's P-47G had never seen combat and had accumulated few flying hours before being surplused off to teach a new generation of mechanics. Heavily damaged during a forced landing after engine failure at an airshow in the early 1970s, the Thunderbolt was put into storage for many years and was only recently completely rebuilt and flown

The Air Museum's P-47G airborne in the capable hands of Don Lykins. Mounting eight .50 calibre machine guns and a variety of underwing stores, the Thunderbolt was capable of creating havoc among enemy ground forces. That big P&W really gulped the fuel and prevented the Thunderbolt (which had nicknames like *Jug*, *T-Bolt*, and *Flying Brick*) from escorting 8th Air Force bombers deep into enemy territory. Additional fuel tanks helped the situation but the Thunderbolt never really became an efficient long-range escort fighter, although it certainly played its part until the Mustang became available. NX3395G (s/n 42-25234) made its first flight after restoration during April 1985 and is painted in the markings of WW2 and Korean ace Walker 'Bud' Mahurin. A rear seat has been added to give passengers the experience of flying in one of America's truly great combat aircraft

Overleaf High above California's central valley, Ray Stutsman's magnificent P-47G restoration poses proudly. Stutsman has acquired a reputation for meticulous warbird restorations but the Thunderbolt is perhaps his crowning effort. Rescued from the junkyard of a Los Angeles aviation eccentric (where it was rotting with several other rare WW2 aircraft), the Thunderbolt underwent a ground-up restoration at Stutsman's shop in Indiana. While taking the T-Bolt completely apart, Ray found a number of curious items—including a bag of cardboard gun barrel plugs, installed when the aircraft left the Curtiss factory!

These pages and overleaf With gear down (left), the Thunderbolt appears to be even more massive. Painted dark olive drab and neutral grey, Stutsman selected the markings of Captain W C Beckham's *Little Demon*

Your basic basket case Thunderbolt. This is just about what every warbird buff would like to find in their front yard for Christmas. It has been acquired by the Yankee Air Corps of Chino, California, a museum responsible for some fantastic restorations and fully capable of getting this neglected Republic P-47M back into the air. NX4477M was acquired from a private owner in Illinois where it had been sitting outside for the last 40 years

Below As mentioned earlier, six Republic P-47D Thunderbolts were returned to the United States in the late 1960s after serving with the air force of Peru. Purchased by vintage warplane collector Ed Jurist, the six T-Bolts were taken to the main Confederate Air Force base at Harlingen, Texas. After being assembled, the machines were flown in formation at several airshows—the first time that a massed P-47 flight had taken place in the States since the early 1950s. Jurist later sold the group to another collector and several of these rare fighters have, unfortunately, been written off in accidents. N47DF is seen having its R-2800 run-up before a flight during January 1974

Steve Hinton in Thunderbolt NX47DD leads an interesting flight of gunslingers: A bubble-top T-Bolt, a razorback P-47G, bubble-top P-51D, and razorback P-51B. NX47DD is one of the ex-Peruvian AF machines and it was nearly destroyed in a takeoff accident at Barstow, California. Passing through several owners (each of whom attempted to rebuild the damaged fighter), the airplane became the property of Stephen Grey. Grey contracted Steve Hinton's Fighter Rebuilders at Chino, California, to bring the old warrior back to life. It took considerable skill and effort: the fuselage was replaced by a unit from a P-47N (apparently a military spare fuselage, for the unit had never been used), while the wing was completely rebuilt. Flying again in mid-1985, Hinton took the big bird to several airshows before it was crated and shipped to Britain—it is now based at Duxford wearing a new paint scheme

'Cats and Corsairs

Left Fighting all the way through the war (including the heroic defence of Wake Island), the Wildcat had little use after the end of hostilities and most were quickly scrapped. However, a few were purchased surplus by private owners and put to work in a variety of menial tasks including crop spraying and aerial survey. N315E (US Navy Bureau Number 47030) is owned by Lex Dupont of Wilmington, Delaware

In recent years over a half dozen Wildcats lurking in barns and hangars have been discovered and restored back to airworthy condition, giving a flying population of about a dozen machines with several more under rebuild. Bob Pond's N47201 is seen at the Imperial War Museum's airfield at Duxford shortly after being painted in a rather fanciful interpretation of the markings of US Navy Commander Butch O'Hare's Wildcat. All flying Wildcats are Eastern-built FM-2s

Left Ex-Grumman test pilot Dick Foote aloft in a dark blue Wildcat (USS *Tulagi* escort carrier markings); N11FE is of interest because its rotund fuselage has been modified to hold four passengers—the 'wide body' fuselage being more than adequate for the task! Looking closely, one can see the smoked windows for the passengers. **Above** One of the better-known Wildcats, is Howard Pardue's FM-2P (a rare photographic variant, note the camera port underneath the wing root). **Overleaf** Another well-known Wildcat is N681S, the Wildcat owned and operated by the Confederate Air Force. Recently rebuilt, the Wildcat is finished in the very attractive pre-war markings of an aircraft serving aboard the USS *Ranger*

Preceding pages Howard Pardue's and the CAF's FM-2 form a most attractive duo over a Texas cloudscape. Both of these machines are often used in CAF airshows to aid in repelling 'attacking' Japanese forces (represented by modified AT-6 and BT-13 trainers used in the film *Tora! Tora! Tora!*). Grumman's logical follow-on to the Wildcat was the very capable F6F Hellcat. Powered by the reliable R-2800 (*the* US Navy engine of WW2), the Hellcat could take on anything the Japanese could put in the air. Hellcats served with Reserve units after the war yet today only about ten remain flyable. One of the nicest of recent restorations is the F6F-5 belonging to Bob Pond. Brought back to life by Steve Hinton's Fighter Rebuilders, N4964W is seen (below) after emerging from the paint shop in a tri-colour camouflage scheme and (right) in formation with The Air Museum's own F6F-5 flown by Mike DeMarino

As the Hellcat was a logical extension of the Wildcat, the Grumman Bearcat was a similar extension of the F6F. The Navy wanted the 'smallest airplane with the biggest engine'. Selecting the tried and true R-2800, the F8F Bearcat combined an elegant, streamlined airframe, with all the available aeronautical technology that had been developed from combat experience. The Bearcat gained the distinction of being one of the finest propeller-driven aircraft ever built—the Bearcat still holds the piston-engine time-to-climb record. Howard Pardue is pictured flying his rare pre-production XF8F-1

One Bearcat currently flies in Britain—Stephen Grey's F8F-2P. NX700H (Buno 121714) is a regular head-turner at airshows—Hugh Proudfoot is seen starting the R-2800 (above) while the insignia to the left is that of VF-11, carried on the cowling of NX700H. The Bearcat on the right is unique—it was built as a civilian aircraft and never saw military service. N700A (designated a G-58B and not an F8F), was used as a high-speed transport by the company's field service representative to call on Navy and Marine units equipped with Grumman jet fighters. Recently purchased by Bob Pond, the 'Cat is seen being exercised by Steve Hinton **overleaf**

Deadly duo. Rick Brickert flies Stephen Grey's
Goodyear-built FG-1D Corsair in the foreground
while Mike DeMarino keeps him company in The
Air Museum's FG-1D. Grey's Corsair had just
completed an overhaul at Fighter Rebuilders and
was on its way to Florida where it was put on a
boat and shipped to Britain for the 1986 airshow
season. The photo above illustrates one of the
main reasons for the Corsair's success and
reliability: the P&W R-2800. It is interesting to
compare the Corsair (designed and flown before
WW2) to the Bearcat. Both machines are powered
by the R-2800 but the Bearcat reflects the
sophistication gained in aeronautical design during
the war

The Air Museum's FG-1D prepares for a flight.
Initially seeing combat with the US Marine Corps
(the Vought Corsair had a problem landing aboard
the Navy's carriers—the stiff gear made a smooth
landing almost impossible and it took some time
to work this problem out), the F4Us quickly
compiled a distinguished combat record during the
island hopping war. The Corsair reflects certain
1930's design points and these include the fabric
covering from the wing spar on back and the
wooden ailerons

The photographs on this page illustrate Howard Pardue's Vought F4U-5N Corsair NX65HP, a fighter that last saw service with the Honduran Air Force. Basically a radar equipped night fighter (the large wing mounted radar pod has been removed), the -5N was a fast and efficient machine, its four 20 mm cannon proving particularly deadly. The formation **overleaf** shows Corsair power at its best: The late Merle Gustafson leads the pack in his F4U-4 followed by Buck Ridley in this F4U-4 and Howard Pardue in his F4U-5N. The Corsair stayed in production longer than any other American piston-engined warplane

Big Hog is a Goodyear-built FG-1D which last
saw active service with the Royal New Zealand
Air Force, an air arm that made extensive use of
the 'bent-wing bird' during WW2. Rescued from
a scrap yard, the airplane was transported back to
the United States and eventually completely
rebuilt by the late Jim Landry. Landry
incorporated many updates in the Corsair,
including metalized wings, extra fuel, and new
avionics—everything needed to make the fighter a
safe and efficient cross-country machine. Landry
was to later die in a skydiving accident

Right Close formation flying at its best. Howard
Pardue (trained as a US Marine Corps fighter
pilot) shows what formation flying is all about.
His FG-1D, NX67HP, was photographed over
Chino, California, during May 1983 from the back
seat of a Beech T-34 Mentor using a 24 mm
lens—that's close! **Overleaf** The FG-1D 'down
and dirty', illustrating the imposing nature of the
Corsair. Around two dozen Corsairs are either
flying or in the process of being restored

One of the few drawbacks to the Corsair during its operational service was the rather poor visibility over that long nose during takeoff and landing. The pilot, positioned roughly mid-fuselage, had a long chunk of aluminium to look past during those two important phases of flight. Once in the air, the pilot of the Corsair was afforded pretty good visibility, as can be seen in this banking view of Howard Pardue's F4U-4, NX68HP—another of the Corsairs returned to the States from Honduras in the late 1970s

Two FG-1Ds in formation: Mike DeMarino leads in the The Air Museum's example (a veteran of the *Baa*, *Baa Black Sheep* television series) while Howard Pardue follows in his Goodyear-built Corsair, painted in the markings of VMF-111. Both of these Corsairs have been modified to carry a passenger directly behind the pilot, the blue-tinted plexiglass of the passenger's windows can barely be detected. Two-seat modifications are becoming more common on the surviving gunfighters—giving someone else a chance to experience the thrill of this type of flying

Mike Wright (above) enjoys some summer flying with the canopy slid back in Don Davis' FG-1D, *Wart Hog* (for some curious reason, the rather elegant Corsair has collected a wide variety of pig-related nicknames). N4715C was completely restored by The Tired Iron Racing Team in Casper, Wyoming, and is flown as both a warbird and as an unlimited air racer (although participating in a leisurely manner). This fighter is also equipped with gas-operated 'machine gun', units that give off a noise convincingly like .50 calibre Brownings and, needless to say, extremely popular with airshow crowds. The classic lines of the FG-1D are shown to the advantage on the left. Flying high above a Texas coastline, this FG-1D was rescued from El Salvador

Overleaf The last combat Corsair: Honduran Air Force mechanics prepare to fire up that country's last Corsair, an F4U-5NL. During 1969, Honduras and Salvador went to war in an incident that has become known as 'The Soccer War', since hostilities took place after a particularly acrimonious match. Reasons for the conflict went much deeper of course, but the two countries were pitted in a brief but deadly battle. Both sides flew Corsairs, the Salvadorian Air Force being beefed up by P-51s smuggled south by American pilots eager for a quick buck. This particular machine, flown by Fernando Soto, shot down two Salvadorian FG-1Ds and a P-51D on one mission, thus becoming the last WW2 piston-engine fighter to record a kill over a similar type of machine

Hawk wings

Left During WW2, airmen and ground crews produced something which is only now becoming to be realized as a very particular form of folk art: the aircraft pin-up. *Sneak Attack* adorns the tail of John Paul's Curtiss P-40E Kittyhawk which is currently being operated in Britain by Ray and Mark Hanna

Hawk over the barren hills of Bakersfield, California. Not so many years ago, the Curtiss P-40 was a distinctly rare shape in the skies over America—only a couple of examples being airworthy. With the increased interest in warbirds, basket case Curtiss fighters have been rebuilt to concourse condition but restorer Bill Destefani was extremely lucky—he found a complete P-40M in a Reno, Nevada, auto museum

Storing his rare find for several years while he completed a couple of Mustang projects, Destefani was able to lavish considerable attention on the Curtiss when the restoration started, virtually every nut and bolt in the fighter being new. A modernized cockpit and instrument panel was installed and the completed Kittyhawk, registered N1232N (which had been used as a cloud seeder in rain making experiments during the 1950s and early 1960s), was finished in a pristine Royal Air Force paint scheme. A farmer by trade, Destefani bases his P-40M and racing Mustangs out of Minter Field, Shafter, California—an old WW2 RAF and USAAF primary training base

Preceding pages and right Same bird, different
feathers. The Air Museum, Chino, California,
needed a flying P-40 to complement their
collection of rare gunfighters so NL45104 was
built up using a bare airframe and parts acquired
from many sources. A late-model P-40N
Warhawk, the Curtiss proved to be a welcome
addition to The Air Museum's growing fleet of
gunfighters and, since completion, has been used
in several movies and television programmes.
After restoration, the P-40N was flown for several
years in a bare metal finish with minimal national
insignia and a hungry set of teeth painted on the
cowling (Steve Hinton is seen piloting the bare
metal bird during the 1983 Minter Field Air
Museum Warbird show). A recent coat of olive
drab paint has given the old fighter a 'new' look,
seen here at the 1986 version of the Minter Field
gathering with Dennis Sanders at the controls

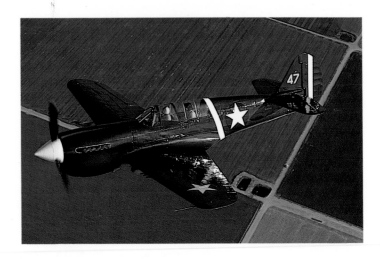

Top left Completely rebuilt from a hulk, this P-40E Kittyhawk, painted up in immediate pre-war US Army Air Corps markings, is the property of P-40 enthusiast Dr Bill Anderson. Almost completely original, N940AK is a fine example of warbird restoration

Left A particularly significant Kittyhawk, this P-40E N41JA has been restored in the markings of the late Robert Prescott, an ace with the American Volunteer Group (AVG or, more popularly, 'Flying Tigers') who also, perhaps more importantly, started Flying Tiger Lines, the first all-cargo airline; it has developed into one of the world's largest operators. N41JA is owned by the parent company and the tail surfaces of the Kittyhawk (painted as a P-40B Tomahawk) have been signed by surviving members of the AVG

Above and overleaf Curtiss TP-40N Warhawk N999CD is owned by Bob Pond and is being flown by Mike DeMarino. The TP-40N was a dual control variant of the Warhawk, with a full instrument panel and set of controls in the rear cockpit, and used as an advanced fighter trainer by the Army. Sometime during the late 1950s/early 1960s, an attempt was made to make the Warhawk look like a single-seater, the complex dual sliding canopies being removed. On exhibition for a considerable period of time at the USAF Museum in Dayton, Ohio, it was declared surplus when a more original P-40E became available and Bob Pond eventually purchased the machine. Seen on a test flight after restoration by Fighter Rebuilders, the aircraft now has its rear seat controls installed

Mike DeMarino in the Curtiss TP-40N and Steve
Hinton in the G-58B Bearcat make for an unusual
formation over the mountains near Chino,
California, during March 1986. A pre-war design,
the Curtiss P-40 series fought on every combat
front and flew right until the end of the war—
compiling an impressive string of victories. The
rugged Curtiss also excelled in the ground attack
role and did particular damage to the German war
machine in North Africa

During the 1960s, aircraft buff Mike Dillon became one of the first to catch 'warbird fever'. Dillon found an abandoned P-40N on an airstrip in Texas, purchased the machine and put blood, sweat, tears and money into getting the corroding pile of metal flying again. He was successful in his endeavours, even though most of his friends told him he was mad. Due to an expanding family, Dillon had to sell his prized N1226N to the Confederate Air Force in Harlingen, Texas, and it still flies with that organization today. Astronaut Joe Engle is seen flying the Warhawk during October 1975

Fearsome teeth highlight John Paul's P-40E on the opposite page while the carefully researched paint scheme on this page is the result of years of work by aircraft restorer Eric Mingledorff. Eric purchased P-40E (an ex-Royal Canadian Air Force fighter, just like most surviving P-40s), and spent several years restoring N1207V to absolutely stock condition. A stickler for detail, Mingledorff picked the rather distinctive paint scheme used by Lt Dallas Clinger and not only traced the pilot, but also his crew chief, to obtain the precise details of 14th Air Force colours and markings. Clinger still has the rudder fabric from his aircraft and Mingledorff was able to create an exact reproduction. After performing at airshows for several years, he reluctantly sold his beautiful Kittyhawk (also pictured overleaf) and is now concentrating on breathing life back into the neglected airframe of an FM-2 Wildcat

P-38s and more hit singles

Lockheed P-38M NL3JB, a two-seat night fighter, during one of its very rare outings from the Champlain Fighter Museum in Mesa, Arizona—home of a fabulous collection of WW1 and WW2 gunfighters, all in flying condition. The airplane is also pictured **overleaf**

Preceding pages and above After many years work and the expenditure of a large amount of money, John Siberman brought a badly wrecked Lockheed F-5 (Lightning photo-reconnaissance variant) back to life and this rare machine is airborne during the 1986 Valiant Air Command airshow in Florida. Difficult to restore, with many complex systems, around four Lightnings are currently under rebuild. N5596V is being flown by Thurston 'Jaybo' Hinyub

This page and overleaf Few warbird types are rarer than the attractive mid-engine fighters produced by the Bell Aircraft Company. The P-39 Airacobra and P-63 Kingcobra both offered the promise of great performance but both failed to deliver—due mainly to the increasing Army demands placed on the airframes, detracting from the original interceptor mission. Today, only two Airacobras and three Kingcobras are airworthy and one of the most familiar to airshow spectators is NL62822, a Kingcobra currently owned by Bob Rieser. Built up during the 1970s as a high performance unlimited air racer by John Sandberg, the much-modified P-63 never did really well against the Mustangs and Bearcats but it was a strong competitor. Passing through several owners since then, the P-63 has acquired a few of its more original features, such as wing tips. But the airplane is so highly modified that it is only representative of the type in general outline. Retaining the bright red/orange paint of its racing days, the Kingcobra is similar to some of the 'pinball' P-63s, heavily armoured aircraft used as flying targets for student gunners and usually painted in bright schemes for obvious reasons

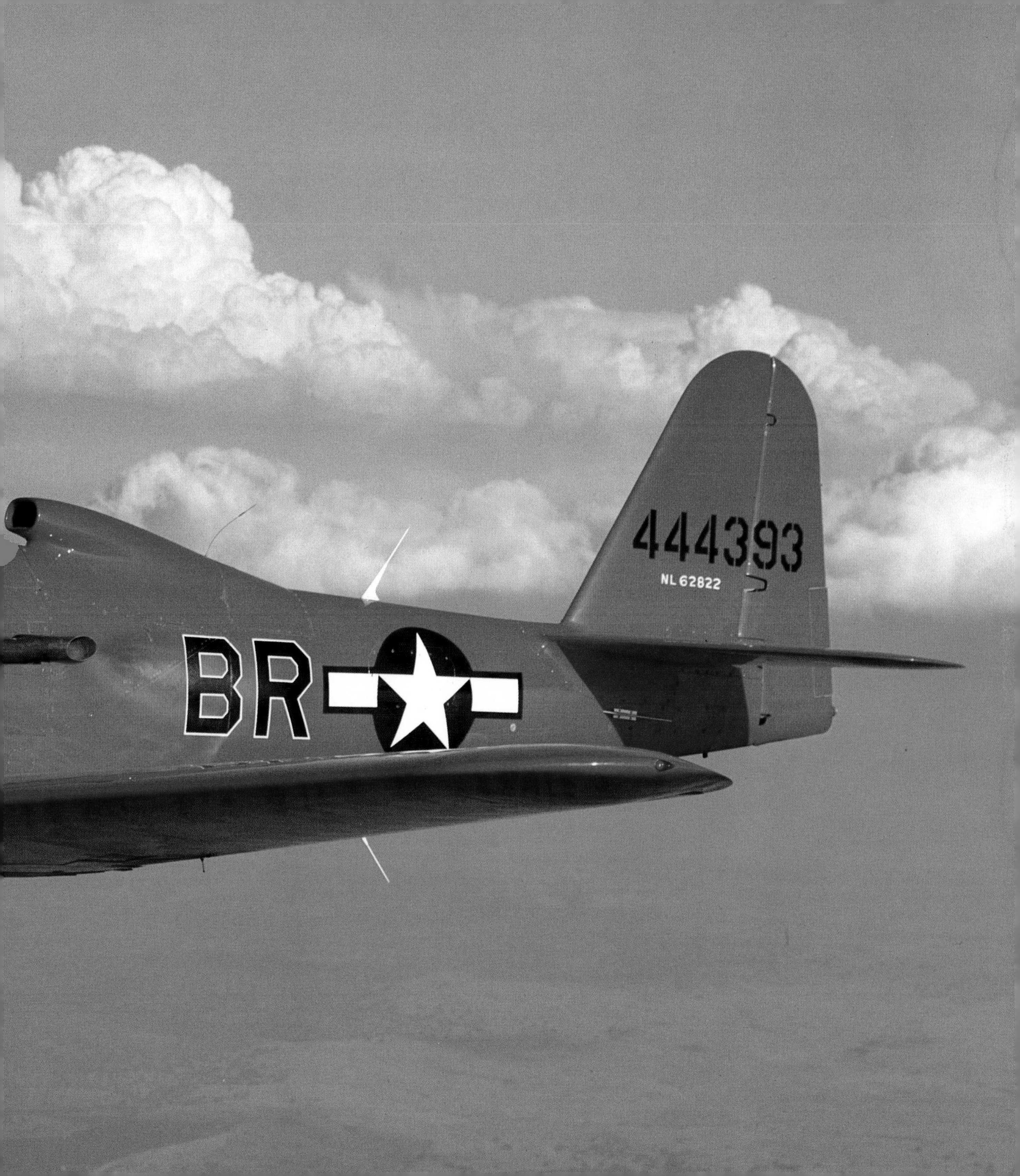
444393
NL 62822
BR

Unique Bell P-63F N6763 has survived two unlimited racing careers and a number of private owners. Currently owned and operated by the Confederate Air Force, the P-63F is seen over a Texas landscape during May 1986. The F variant of the Kingcobra was a one-off attempt by Bell to update and improve the basic design. The airframe was generally cleaned up to offer better streamlining and a much larger vertical tail was added to improve stability but, with several more advanced designs to chose from, the Army Air Force did not proceed with the P-63F and N6763 became the last of Bell's propeller-driven fighters

Right With gear just starting to retract, The Air Museum's ultra-rare Mitsubishi A6M5 Zero is seen shortly after takeoff from Chino Airport during May 1983. Back in the early 1950s, Air Museum founder Ed Maloney obtained two Zero airframes that the military was in the process of dumping. The planes had been used for evaluation by the Navy and then simply junked—one Zero had its wings cut off before Maloney could rescue it. The two airframes passed from location to location over the years as Maloney attempted to find a permanent home for his museum—a museum created before public interest in veteran and vintage warplanes had begun. At this time in the museum's history, there was no thought given to making a Zero airworthy but that was to change during the 1970s

As Maloney's son, Jim, grew into adulthood, he became very interested in his father's collection of aircraft. Developing into an excellent pilot and mechanic, the younger Maloney began to get some of the collection back into the air—where it belonged. Accompanied by boyhood friend Steve Hinton and an enthusiastic band of volunteers, the museum began to slowly grow and prosper. One of the most radical restorations was the A6M5—a rebuild that took several years, lots of support, and money. The entire wing was respared (the original alloy had rotted), the 1130 hp Sakae 21 radial engine was restored to running order (no small feat since it is the *only* Japanese WW2 aero engine still flying), and all systems were Americanized to make operation of the Zero more practical and safer. Obviously not flown every day, the Zero is one of the highlights of the annual Planes of Fame airshow at Chino where it is seen in company gith some of its WW2 enemies

The Supermarine Spitfire remains a rare bird in American skies but several examples are currently flying and a couple more are under restoration. One of the more regular Spitfire airshow visitors is Bill Greenwood and his T Mk 9, a two-seat fighter trainer variant of the single-seat machine. N308WK is maintained in beautiful condition and operated out of Aspen, Colorado, from an airfield 6000 ft above ground level. Built for the Irish Air Corps, an extensive modification saw the front cockpit moved forward about a foot and a second

seat with full instrumentation and controls installed on the aircraft's spine. One T Mk 9 has been converted back to its original single-seat configuration in Britain for Stephen Grey (at considerable expense) but Greenwood currently plans to keep his machine in its training configuration. The aircraft, in the flying shot, is being piloted by Earl Ketchen during May 1984 and who, unfortunately, was killed in the crash of a P-51D shortly afterwards

Former enemies. After the movie *Battle of Britain*, about 16 ex-Spanish Air Force Hispano Ha.1112 fighters (a Merlin-powered Spanish-built variant of the famous Messerschmitt Bf 109) were imported to the States. Most of those restored to flying condition are no longer flying and for good reason—nearly all have succumbed to landing and takeoff accidents. Warbird enthusiast Dr Bill Harrison obtained one of the Hispanos and, after he had accumulated over 50 hours flying time in the fighter, was kidded about being the highest time Hispano pilot without an accident. Unfortunately this did not hold true very long for, after this October 1977 photo was taken, the aircraft groundlooped and tore out its landing gear. The damaged airframe was eventually sold to British warbird collector Robs Lamplough who spent several years restoring it. After a couple of flights the airplane (guess what) was groundlooped and suffered severe damage. Last we heard, the Hispano is being rebuilt back to WW2 configuration (complete with a German DB605 engine) for a new owner in New Zealand. The Hispano is pictured in formation with the CAF's P-40N Warhawk

Few will deny that one of the last British propeller-driven fighters is also one of the most graceful. The Hawker Sea Fury has found great popularity among American warbird collectors and most of the surviving flyable airframes are now in the States. N260X was imported from Australia in the 1960s and enjoyed a very brief (and unspectacular) air racing career before lapsing into dereliction. Eventually purchased by airline pilot Ellsworth Getchell, N260X was restored to mint condition over a period of several years and finished in attractive Royal Australian Navy markings

N260X, finished as RAN WH587, is seen in a couple of different poses during the 1984 Madera, California, Gathering of Warbirds airshow. The big Sea Fury is one of the fastest of the piston-engine fighters and is enjoying great popularity at Reno—especially when re-engined with the massive Pratt & Whitney R-4360 radial like *Dreadnought* and *Furias*. The bright blue aircraft **overleaf** is a Hawker Fury, a land-based variant built for the air force of Iraq during the early 1950s. With naval gear removed, Iraq operated several dozen of the fighters. Warbird collectors David Tallichet and Ed Jurist scored a major coup in the late 1970s when they obtained two dozen Furies and tons of spare parts from Iraq. Transported to Florida, some of the Furies have been sold, restored, and are now flying. Michael Mock is seen piloting N21SF, an aircraft he and his father restored. Adding such custom touches as brass landing gear door linings, the Fury is painted in the dark blue markings of the Royal Australian Navy's aerobatic team which operated the type in the late 1950s

Just jets

One of the finest flying examples of America's early jet fighters is Dave Zeuschel's North American F-86F Sabre seen, (left) as it rolls over the top of the Mustang camera ship and, (above) prepared for its next flight from Zeuschel's home airfield of Van Nuys, California (where the Sabre had one time been based with the ANG)

What's it take to have your own jet fighter? Well, to start with, you have to find one! Zeuschel found his rare Sabre carefully disassembled and stored in an old barn high in a mountainous area under a gradually thickening layer of dust and bird droppings. Carefully transporting his find back to his workshop, he spent several years bringing the fighter back to airworthy condition. A major help in the project was the discovery of a small warehouse full of new Sabre spares—just a few days before the parts were scheduled for scrapping!

This page and overleaf Zeuschel had always
admired the colourful markings of the 4th Fighter
Group's Sabres in Korea so when it became time
to paint N86Z he chose the simple but attractive
markings of the F-86 flown by MiG-ace Major J J
Jabara, America's first jet ace. Jabara scored 1½
kills during WW2 and then went on to rack up 15
more (see last page) over enemy MiG-15s during
the Korean War. He achieved his fifth and sixth
MiG kill on 20 May 1951. Jabara was killed in an
automobile accident in 1966

Above Steve Hinton is seen flying John Sandberg's F-86F Sabre during the May 1984 Planes of Fame airshow. This particular aircraft, NX86F, was rescued from Peru after it had been withdrawn from the Peruvian Air Force. Transported to Los Angeles, the aircraft was completely rebuilt to become one of the very few original American-built Sabres on the civil register

Below Canadair Sabre N86CD is seen after having emerged from the Unlimited Aircraft Limited restoration facility at Chino in early 1986. The aircraft will be used by ace aerobatic pilot Bob Hoover for a series of airshow displays

A naked N86Z (above) during a test flight in June 1983. Registering a civil jet fighter is not an easy task, the Federal Aviation Administration remembering the disastrous crash of a Sabre into an ice cream parlor over a dozen years ago with resultant heavy loss of life. The Canadair Sabre (below) in *Luftwaffe* markings is how the restorations of some jet fighters begin

Overleaf N86F in the markings of Aviation Systems International, as test pilot Skip Holm heads the Sabre into a rapidly setting sun firing the underwing Frank Sanders Smokewinders